I0527044

Moral Compass

WRITTEN BY: DANIEL PENALOZA, AKA DLOZA

Copyright 2017

License Notes: All rights reserved and solely belonging to said author known here Daniel E. Penaloza. This book or any portion thereof is not to be reproduced or used in any manner without the written and signed permission from said author.

This book is licensed for your personal enjoyment only. This book is not to be re-sold nor copied in any way, shape or form via any means. Please respect the literary work here presented and written by said author.

WORDS FROM THE AUTHOR

Many of us venture thru life searching deep within our soul for answers to questions that are redundant, but never get old. Morally we are equally subject to the same, making decisions in life that are cold as ice, who is to ever blame. Our actions bring forth snow filled frigid nights that mimic winter weather from the artic NORTH skyline, only to later burn from misconceived notions, that raise the temperature with heat filled emotions, all expressed via word of mouth, unsettling thoughts set in, morally crashing, heading SOUTH. We feel that change is best, so we turn & focus to the WEST. A new beginning awaits within the valley of sunsets. Gold filled mountains, cactus infused deserts, the feeling of hope & opportunity is well worth the effort. A moral change of heart transcends, fasting for the origin of what made us never ends. Laying on the beach at night while counting stars, indulging on the Ocean breeze from the Atlantic seas that lie EAST, cleanse & heal emotional scars. It is where I find my peace, the roots from where I've sprung Is where I feel at ease. Where ever your Moral Compass takes you in life be sure to fulfil your desires & dreams, regardless of it bringing you happiness or strife.

Table of Contents

You can travel through
life serving as societies
mat under a door,
Or lead with your cape,
striking down adversaries
with your sword.
MATADOR

Dloza

Addicting like an opiate,
my side effects are unconventional,
but never unfortunate.
Catering to your needs with
passion, euphoric.
I can't be your Superman, I favor
the Dark Knight, mysterious, yet
still heroic.
I go down smooth & sweet like fine
wine or distinctly aged whiskey.
Not a day goes by without you
expressing how much you miss me.
Dloza

In life you will be confronted with scenarios that will require you to pull the plug inducing a Flatline. The message received by this will be loud & clear, no need to keep providing a life line..
Dloza

Thirsty from a drought derived from the lack of attention.
The void becomes nonexistent, as it floods with affection filled precipitation.
Quench your thirst selectively, satisfying your palate may compromise who you are unexpectedly...
Dloza

Maybe it's the thin sleek heel,
Maybe it's the various designs revealed,
Maybe it's the contour of the calves when a woman kneels.
Whatever the case maybe, nothing drives my attention more so than,
STILETTO HEELS...
Dloza

Her smile lights up rooms,
mimicking incandescent candles
that are placed in the hallways of
strategic ballrooms.
An empress amongst mankind,
her pure, untainted nature has
many claiming she's from the gods,

simply DIVINƐ...
Dloza

My flame is slowly dying,
evaporating.
It's weakness is evident from the thirsty
wick that is fading.
Darkness hijacks the soul without
hesitating,
The denial of fuel & neglect have met,
collaborating.
It's vital & an essential need, fuel your fire
in life, don't let it run out of
KEROSENE..

Align yourself in life with the willing &
capable.
Barricade yourself from the deceitful &
mentally unstable.
Grow your relationships with trust,
loyalty and respect that is favorable.
Unlike the biblical tales derived from the
stories of
CAIN & ABEL..
Dloza

Never fantasize over
dreams that rally
around stars who are
closer to Venus rather
than Mars.
Stay within the realm of
relativity, find your
common denominator
that flows with earth's
given gravity,
that will be the
instrumental
key...
Dloza

Venturing thru life often mimics the uncertainty you feel when driving over black ice.
At any given moment situations may change.
Some will be sweet while others will become sour.
Some will lose, others will gain.
The goal is to remain stable on any given hour, never fall to any demands insisting that you change...
Dloza

Never sure about what I desire for each day.
On modestly cool sunny days
I pray that the gods bring down thunder & hail infested
rains.
I book lavish vacations, only to seek out local gyms to
release my disingenuous affliction.
My needs for pleasure & pain have joined to fuel my
commingled addiction.
I have changed, nothing will ever be the same...
Dloza

You use to B

You use to be my sunshine during the cloudiest of days.
Now you're just a mere shadow that I wish to never claim.
You use to be my flashlight during a power outage.
Now you've confirmed everything that I've initially feared & doubted.
You use to be the beat that increased my hearts excitement.
Now you've become toxic, I've come to terms & will not fight it...

Dloza

Jammin out to a slow smooth tempo, laced with a cooling rhythm that stirs the imagination & nourishes the soul.

The fluctuation of the beats reminds me of the times when I called home the streets.

Ill willed parties were always prevalent,

Not much of a choice when families make you feel irrelevant.

Despite of the hurdles that were set to test my capability,

I've remained calm and leaped over them with relentless stamina & unforeseen Agility...

Dloza

You "R"

You are the beacon of light that guides me thru turbulent dreams at night.

You are the majestic force that draws to me like a magnet that's been placed next to my stainless steel sword.

You are the petals to my rose, and the thorns that discipline me for reasons that only God knows.

You are the icing on my cake, staying sweet & irresistible even when I make a mistake.

You are everything I've ever dreamed of & wanted.

My skeletons have been exposed, the closet doors have been closed.

I've started a new chapter, wishing only to live happily ever after...

Dloza

RED ~ Stop, observe, listen. Cease your forward progress, abide by your souls intuitions.

AMBER ~ Proceed with various options, yield to voices that are outspoken & linger within your conscious.

GREEN ~ Accelerate yourself to what suits you best, never settle for anything less...
Dloza

I like the fullness of your lips
and the way you shake that a$$ while
seductively swaying your hips.
I'm losing track of time, suffering from
blurred vision, you've become my new
found addiction,
losing my f*cking mind.
You stir thoughts within me, should I seek
medical attention or let you be the judge
with anticipation of a favorable
plea.
You place me into a trance when you
whisper into my ear, I will never reject,
instead I shall adhere & welcome your
advance.
Your wishes have become my commands.
Justification of this will vary, respect is
all I demand, I hope you
understand.
Dloza

Sophistication is a mind set that requires discipline.

Circumstances will arise that may pose an imminent threat.

Fighting over principle is a lost cause, tripping over nonsense will expose a character flaw.

Stay true to your caliber, contradicting what you've established will label you as dissident, mimicking the behavior of a desperate scavenger will become meaningless...

Dloza

I see the light shining through the greens,
It's mystical, mesmerizing, almost
obscene.

Simulating the gateways to heaven, it
warms me, calms me down, bringing sanity
& tranquility, dispersing any unforseen
aggression, something I've always looked for
but have never found,
my unfulfilled
obsession...

Dloza

My thoughts & goals ride high, choosing not to settle.
I will not be
denied.
Success has been deemed inevitable.
My flight pattern has become favorable.
The storms have cleared,
free from any turbulence or chaotic windshear, proceed
with the shifting of gears.
Running on high octane, throttled into the triple digits.
Obstructions don't exist, even the skies have realized it's
become impossible to govern my limits, no need to resist.
The jury is still out.
I'm aware of those who've aligned with me & the few who
remain on the fence while dwelling on misperceived
doubts.
Dloza

I roll like an island's summer
eve.
Hot & humid, laced with a coconut
scented oceanic breeze.
An oasis undisturbed from today's
society,
falling off the grid, a lifestyle
thought of as a myth is now my
reality.
A castaway is where my heart &
soul roams, distant from conflict or
friction, residing amongst the
unknown.
Dloza

Inhale, exhale, revived from suffocating,
I've fallen under a spell as the Witches begin
deliberating.
I'm bleeding from the soul, a tourniquet
has been applied, slowing down the blood
loss & obstructing the flow.
The extraction from venomous entities has
been executed, need not search for old
fashion remedies, the potency from any
strike has become innocuous,
diluted.
Dloza

God hands me a shot of pain, I indulge on it like aromatic wine or red carpet Champagne.

Lucifer applauds, granting me the same, I turn it down, no need to add fuel to the fire, I'm content with the current flame.

Sometimes life's most vital lessons are best digested & absorbed by accepting the unforeseen while swallowing the sword...

Dloza

Waking up to another senseless tragedy,
the mentally ill have struck again adding to
their claimed fatalities.
Seeking answers, contemplating on viable
solutions,
The sickness will continue to spread,
into the souls who fall for sinister illusions.

They will only listen to the voices in their
head.
We must seek them out thru society &
social media, not watch & wait for them
to act instead...
Dloza

I LICK MY WOUNDS, NOURISH, THEN LAY DOWN.
FIGHTING TURBULENCE & WAKE FROM DAILY
STORMS,
I SHALL NOT DROWN.
I'VE RISEN ABOVE EXPECTATIONS,
NEVER FALLING SHORT TO COMDENATION.
I WILL SEEK, CONQUER & REIGN.
NEVER FLUCTUATING LIKE A DEFECTIVE
APPARATUS.
I WILL REMAIN CONSISTENT,
ALWAYS IN THE
GAME...
DLOZA

Unique, almost obsolete, trendsetting, underrated, despite it all I'm still collaborating.
Creator of the unheard, basking within my riches, dissing all naysayers & dysfunctional B$tches, vocalizing crystal clear not hypothetically slurred, as perceived by those who are in need of stitches, some what disturbed.
I choose to digress, not in search of stress or welcome it non the less, always wishing all who hate the very best..

Dloza

Midnight Licorice

Unwrapped at midnight after
Some dinner & wine.
Body language confirmed,
We are now seeing eye to
Eye.
Hands come alive,
In full motion,
Fingers lead the way
Spreading chocolate
Scented lotion.
Tongue & cheeks cross
Paths seductively.
Cherry flavored licorice
Introduced & used
PROVOCATIVELY...

DLOZA

Hunger for success like a wolf,

Provide & nourish like a sheep,

Protect & defend like a lion who never sleeps...

Dloza

Tossing, turning, contaminating thoughts,

Unable to speak,

Slurring.

Visions of my queen filter through my

Incandescent dreams.

She hovers just below the trees,

Beckoning to be grabbed & pulled

Towards me.

I reach out to her,

Run my fingers through the air.

I awaken in a cold sweat,

Realizing no one is

There...

Dloza

Thirsty, hungry, reborn
by the Apocalypse I
must be.
Bloodshot eyes, walking
side to side, I'm often
viewed awkwardly.
Zombie is the calling I
hear that travels thru
buildings & trees.
Chasing then eating the
living is what I desire &
need...

Falling from the skies,

Tears from Mother Nature's Eyes,

Nourish the young and old,

Landing on various landscapes

Within organic souls.

Replenishing what's dehydrated,

Contemplation is nonexistent,

Its sheer necessity often misconceived,

Commonly underrated despite its

PERSISTENCE...

AGUA

DLOZA

Relationships with others will

Blossom or fade.

Provide nourishment,

Keep them well fed,

Or let them dry out & fall by

The wayside instead.

Cultivating on contaminated

Soil will only produce

Disappointment & unwanted

TURMOIL...

DLOZA

Cracking, snapping, derived from the lack of
Napping.
Snacking while fasting, contradicting goals,
Slacking.
Where am I, what am I doing & why,
I'm out of control, can't keep track,
losing my f*$king mind...
Insomniac

Bleeding, leading, from a flooding river of

Red is never misleading.

Quivering while remaining resilient and

Optimistic.

Dusk sets in as my heart rate descends,

The vision of heavens gates have become

Realistic.

I awaken from this insane dream,

Roll over and tuck back in nestled

Within the arms of my QUEEN...

DLOZA

Unloading my clip on a regular basis keeps my precision on cue, the adrenaline rush is endless. The recoil is addicting, Heat off the muzzle is calming yet somewhat conflicting...

Dloza

Love the way you're smelling
tonight.
That sleek silk dress showcases
your curves, drawing me to pursue
a bite.
You're a hybrid, a unique mix.
A tall glass of beautiful with a dash
of cuteness, the true definition of
bliss.
#CUTIEFUL
Dloza

I love the taste of your lips, let
me digress and gather my wits.

I'm in a trance when we lock
eyes, I have no control, you have
seduced my mind, body & soul,
I cannot deny...

Dloza

B.M.W

Beware of the wolf in sheep's
clothing.
Mask your intentions & thoughts
accordingly.
Watch for the shifting of tides then
strike,
Unknowingly...
Dloza

Treading through the waters of the Snake River is challenging. The adrenaline rush is chilling, never ending, inducing tranquility & feelings I've never felt or have come to know, beyond comprehending.

Interacting with nature is the addiction of my mind, body and soul. I crave, desire & value it more so than gold. It calms me, brings me sanity, lights my fire and provides me with youth keeping me from the old amicably...

Dloza

YOU : Fronting, portraying, perpetrating,
delaying.
ME : Standing steady, always ready, never,
hesitating.
YOU : Always barking, falling short of biting, intimidation
is your game never
fighting.
ME : Down for whatever, using methods that never fall short
of clever, stimulating blood flow,
inciting.
Your glow is fading, lackluster, as mine is illuminating
under lights blazing onto a diamond filled
cluster.
Dloza

I stare awkwardly into the night, wondering where my Queen lies this evening, she is missing, out of sight.

She calls securing my trust & loyalty. It comes off as priceless, comforting, an act of royalty...

Dloza

"Words from the Serpent"

Gentle, sleek, often coming off as meek.

Not registering under any given apparatus,

sound the alarm, even though I mean no

harm, neglecting the fact of my current

status.

Keep calm, proceed on, no need to fret.

You have me misunderstood,

have no fear, I pose no threat..

Dloza

Thunder & lightning settles in, the Gods are angry let the chaos begin.

The daunting light spectacle conquers the skyline. Crackling sounds become the audible outline as the dancing of cool air and a warm breeze begin rotation.

Lifting objects from the ground, snapping trees without consideration...

Dloza

Hot, dry & somewhat aggravated, as the temperature is rising while the heat is elevating.

A chess game during an excursion begins, giving way to manipulation, no telling how it will end.

King, Queen, Bishop, or Pawn, strategical placed, solidifies your control, giving the disadvantaged no choice but to move on, winning never gets old...

Dloza

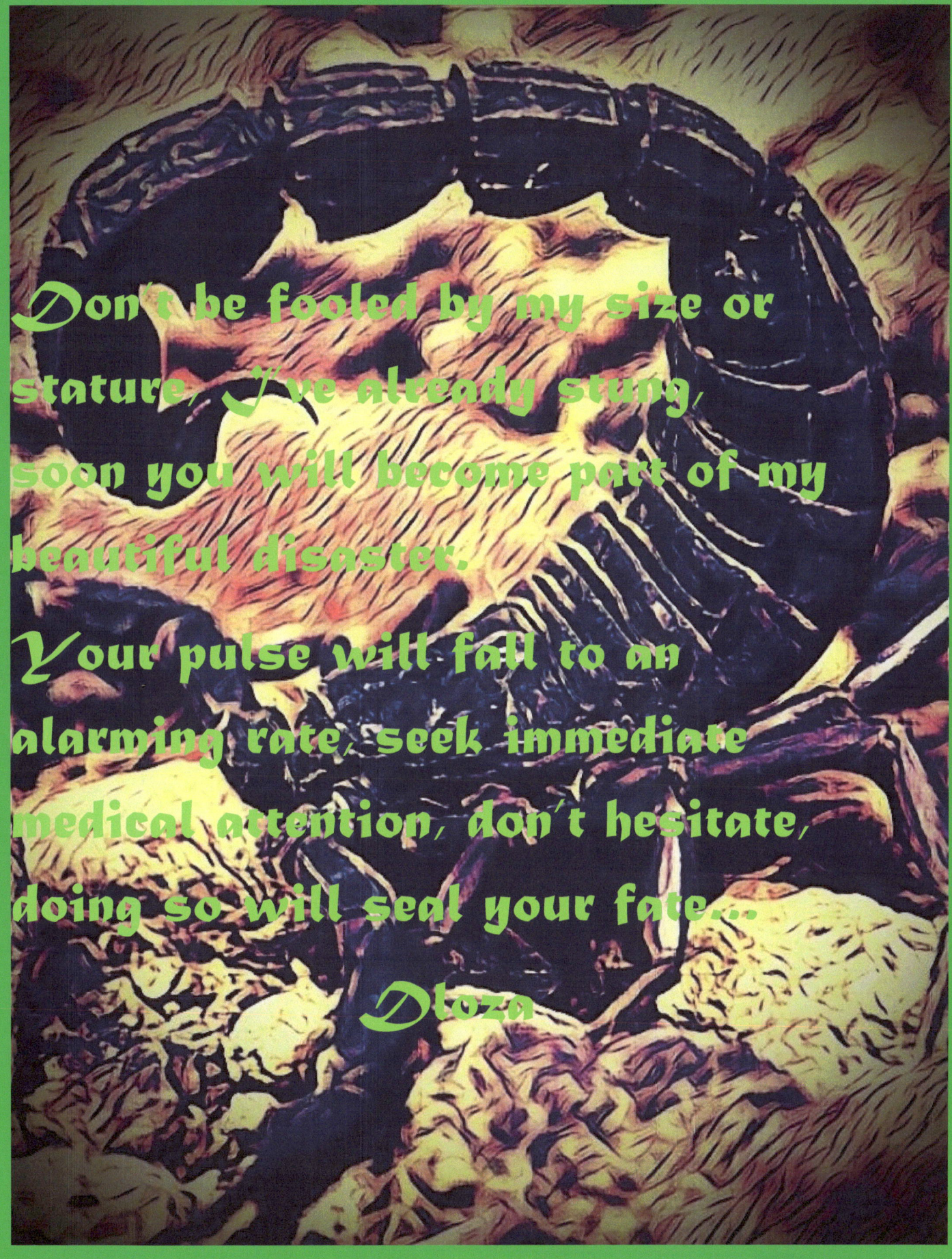

Don't be fooled by my size or stature, I've already stung, soon you will become part of my beautiful disaster.

Your pulse will fall to an alarming rate, seek immediate medical attention, don't hesitate, doing so will seal your fate...

Dloza

Running rampant through the greens,
lavish corn fields, whiskey stills,
surrounded by lumber mills,
the Mississippi Dream.
Amish settlements clearly visible & always
prevalent.
Purification amongst the social scheme, not
highly popular, falling short of relevant or
so it seems.
The diversity of humanity, distorts some
minds as they come to terms while seeking
sanity.

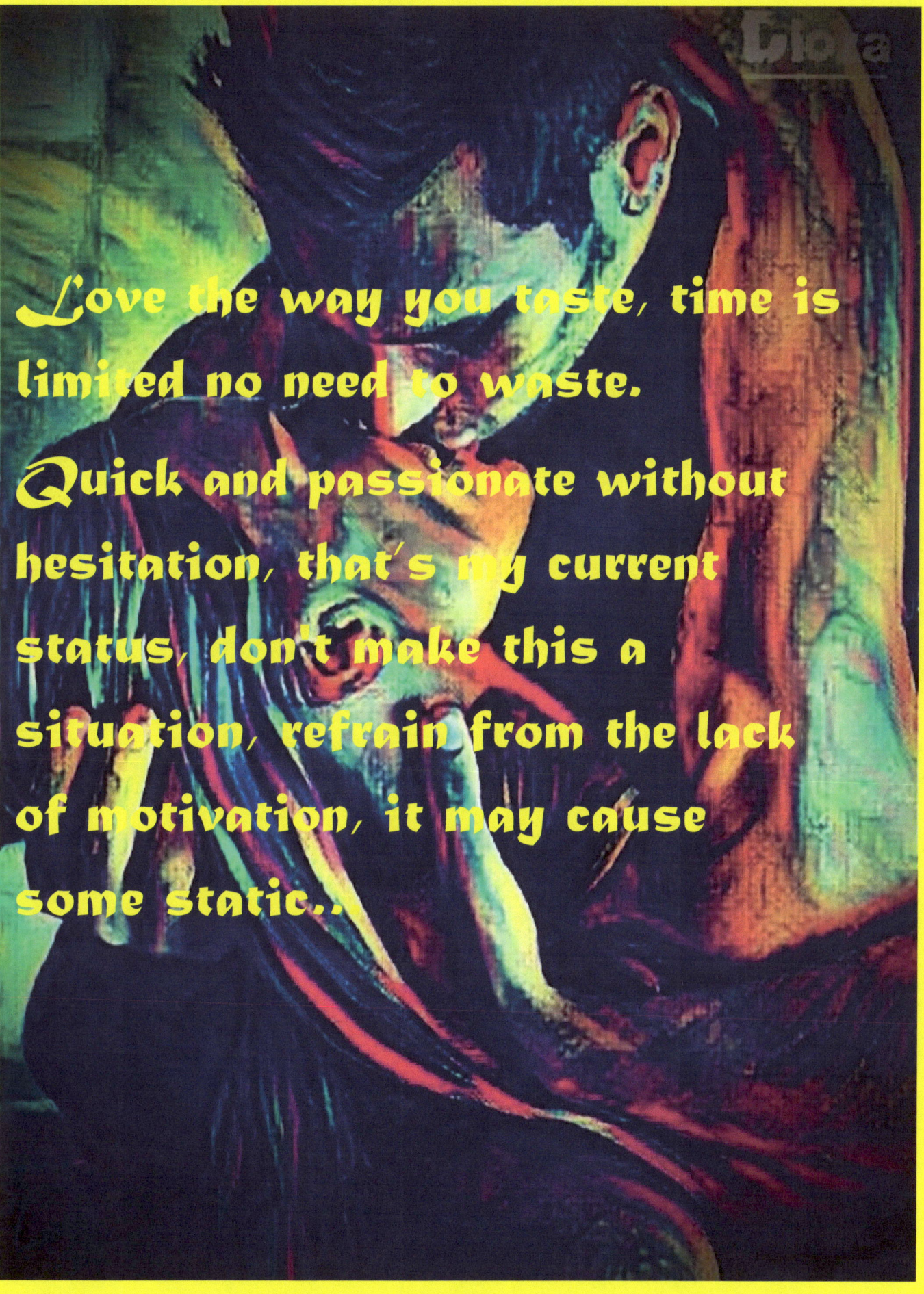

Love the way you taste, time is limited no need to waste.

Quick and passionate without hesitation, that's my current status, don't make this a situation, refrain from the lack of motivation, it may cause some static..

Precipitation & gloom, lingers at dawn
after haunting the moon.
The sun is dealt the same hand from a
different deck.
Darkness hovers, ominous clouds drift in
while casting threats.
The struggle between sunlight & the
billowing mass of haze,
delivers a catalytic effect, rotting the
weather as the skies decay...
SOMBER DAYZ

The sun is setting on the mountains, lighting the waters & governing the horizons.

The visual spectrum shifts, shadows vaporize into a forgotten mist.

A mixture of colors is on display, captivating flawlessly, dancing in disarray...

Dloza

Dancing while biting at your neck,
"Despasito"
Leading into miniscule kisses step
by step,
"Despasito"
Walking with you as the evening
ends, pondering if a new life may
begin,
"Despacito"
Life is marathon filled with
obstacles,
no need to sprint, you will come off
looking lost & somewhat
methodical...
"Despacito"

It was a splendid evening, the exchange of articulate dialogue left me wondering, transcending into a dream, if she only knew what lingers inside, it would make her scream & hide, my true colors would be revealed, Jekyll & Hyde. It's time to part ways, a farewell kiss comes into play. I fight back the urge, stealing her last breath would bring an apocalyptic surge...

Dloza

Incline, decline, rewind, in the end
we always rise.
What's mine is yours, what's yours
is mine.
Everything now is intertwined.
Rollin as a team, focused on
progression,
receiving blessings with the green,
our new found obsession.
Nothing stands in our way.
Committed, focused & driven,
is how we've been known to play...

An angel has fallen under my spell. She is handled accordingly from what I can see & foretell. Despite governing myself as a gentleman, It is she who has taken over aggressively, indulging on my body to satisfy her sickness, I have become her medicine...

Dloza

Teflon

Viscosity is my self induced trait,

not even the mightiest of trains can evoke friction while

carrying their heaviest freight.

Slick as can be,

I dodge unconventional screams & scenarios awkwardly.

Proclaimed stories & tales of me,

have many questioning their mental state & status of

sanity...

The blades on my Dorian
swords slice & dice.
Cross the line then you will be
paying the price.
I'm an outcast, misfit, align with
anarchy, bloodline is hereditary
from an Assassin's Creed

Mahogany

Walking through dimly lit downtown streets, adjacent to
mahogany laced fences that have become shields to
penthouse suites.

I cross the reflection from a silver coin that's been left &
lost.

I pick it up and continue with my walk.

This practice is a mere reflection of how I've been raised &
taught.

Finding the love of my life occurred in a similar fashion.

It's a trend I've developed, recovering what's been left &
misplaced has become my passion...

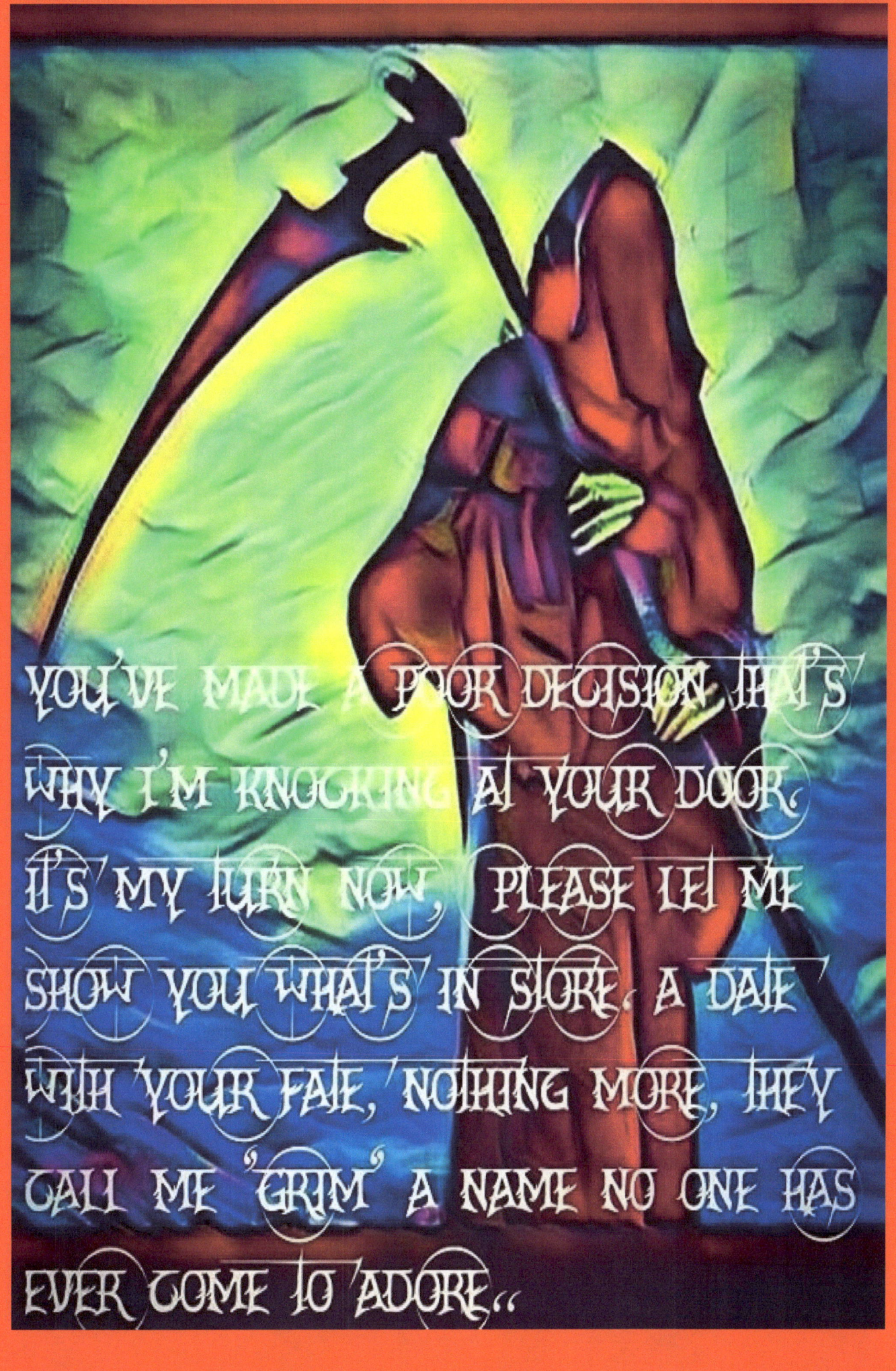

Flowing thru the Mic. with my cool, calm &
collected flow,
I stagnate, digress, and fall back into my
tempo.
Cold as Ice, I'm often perceived as not
being nice,
It's the fire they sense after being caught
up in their lies.
Terminated from existence, is the
prescription that leaves them empty,
dysfunctional & seeking medical assistance...

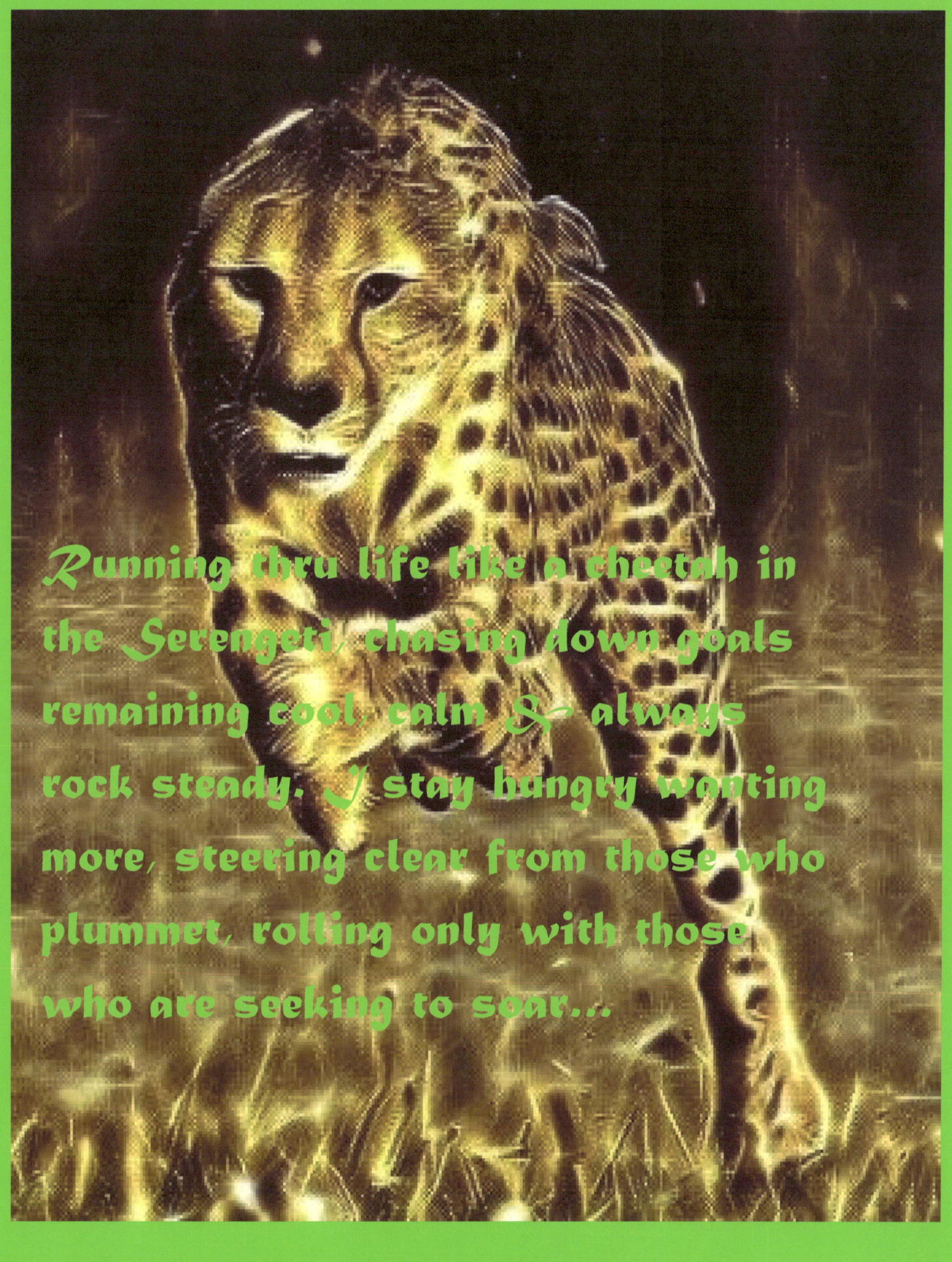

Running thru life like a cheetah in the Serengeti, chasing down goals remaining cool, calm & always rock steady. I stay hungry wanting more, steering clear from those who plummet, rolling only with those who are seeking to soar...

Walking, observing, acknowledging visuals at
times can become
disturbing.
The mentally intoxicated, commingled with
the mentally aggravated, joining hands,
planning societies future
plan.
The rebirth of Gotham has formed, stay
vigilant & Informed,
welcome to the modern day

norm...
Dloza

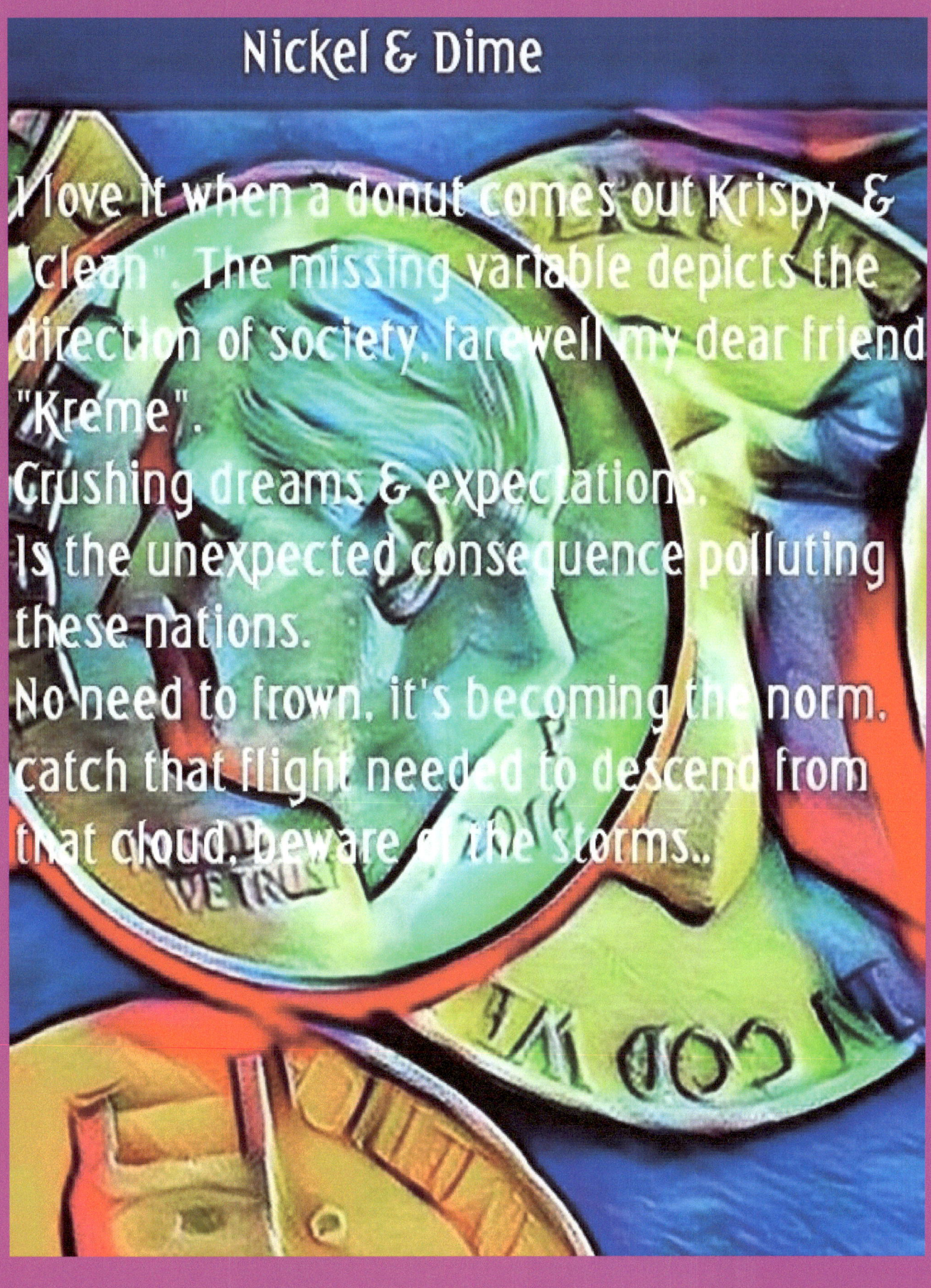

Nickel & Dime

I love it when a donut comes out Krispy & "clean". The missing variable depicts the direction of society, farewell my dear friend "Kreme".

Crushing dreams & expectations,
Is the unexpected consequence polluting these nations.
No need to frown, it's becoming the norm.
catch that flight needed to descend from that cloud, beware of the storms..

Incognito

Our presentation is surreal & genuine,
We are kind by nature, having no reason to
hide or pretend.

We posses the purest of souls, with
skeletons residing deep within the closets
of the unknown.

At times

our demeanor transcends, hiding the

carbon fiber composites from family &

friends.

We live partially in a state of incognito,

periodically crossing paths amongst the

few that are aware and already know...

To all the beautiful, Mothers, Step Mothers, and some Grandmothers who have taken on the primary role in a child's life, this day is for you. We appreciate your patience, guidance, and protection. Your presence is with us from our "First" to "Final" pulse, we are a meer shadow, a mirrored reflection of you, even when we're at our worst...

Bound by thoughts & dreams,
Everyone is looking for their King or Queen.
Cutting out colored paper hearts is a gesture that is
welcomed & embraced by many from the start.
As fading sets in, the greetings with open arms ends, the
slicing & dicing begins, shredding them apart.
Be mindful of reality, steer clear from anticipated empathy,
falling to your knees in tears, exposes desperation, instilling
fear, not the supportive cheer.
Stand strong, refrain from lusting over what is petty.
You will gain respect, a far cry from those who dismiss you

as

EMOTIONAL CONFETTI...

Dloza

I hate you,

I love you,

I can't live without you.

You make me roar,

Show my teeth,

Yet I still crave you,

Wanting more,

Without you I cannot sleep,

This I will always confess,

Never Ignore...

Dloza

I COME & GO,

nostalgically predicting my moves is a farce, no one will

ever know.

I slide & glide on dance floors, countless river edges and

various mountain slopes.

I sip & slurp,

on liquids that are known to be toxic & foreign to anything

that currently reigns on this God given earth.

Life hands you a short & brief pamphlet. Learn it, digress

from it, or take it by

it's horns & just handle it...

Dloza

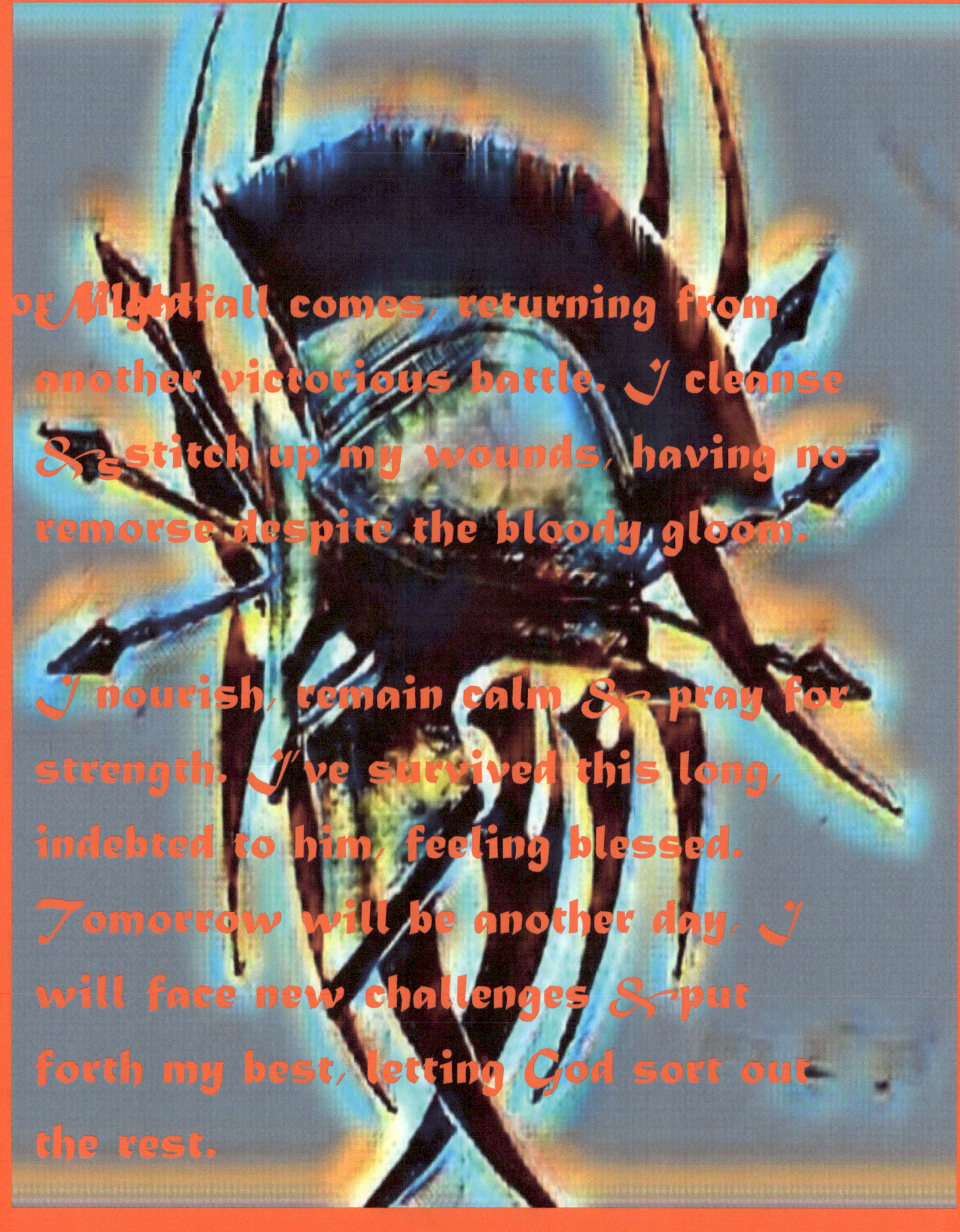

As Nightfall comes, returning from another victorious battle. I cleanse & stitch up my wounds, having no remorse despite the bloody gloom.

I nourish, remain calm & pray for strength. I've survived this long, indebted to him, feeling blessed.

Tomorrow will be another day, I will face new challenges & put forth my best, letting God sort out the rest.

www.ingramcontent.com/pod-product-compliance
Lightning Source LLC
Chambersburg PA
CBHW041536240626
47164CB00002B/28